Thank you for buying this book.

I hope you find the message within this short book meaningful. I know if you practice The Principles of The Rose you will make a difference in the garden.

----- Rick Dove

NOT ALL ROSES BLOOM ON THE SAME DAY

A message of hope for parents, teachers, and leaders.

By Rick L. Dove

(NOT ALL ROSES BLOOM ON THE SAME DAY)

Copyright © 2014 by (Rick Dove)

978-0-9862819-1-4

Dedicated to three of the most influential people in my life:

My wife and best friend **Mary**

My first consultant **Grandma Dove**

My teacher and guide **Ken Blanchard**

Table of Contents

Forward

Hi, I'm Rick Dove, the author of this book. I teach at a university and work as a leadership consultant. You might say that I came by my profession somewhat naturally. You see, my grandmother was my first leadership consultant. As a direct result of our conversations that took place over a small rose garden and her kitchen table, I learned principles that have made a profound difference in my life, and in the lives, both personal and professional, of thousands of students, managers, employees, and families.

I have written this book in order to share the insights and wisdom my grandmother shared with me many years ago.

We live in the age of the critic. We are shrouded by the constant noise of unbridled criticism. We are exposed to criticism daily on TV, internet, and radio. We read the critics' reviews in newspapers and magazines. Unfortunately, we face a lot of criticism at work and in our families. In this environment, we can become extremely critical of ourselves.

Often it seems as if the critic gets more attention than someone who goes out and experiments with a new idea or goes the extra mile to make a difference. I believe the exposure to constant criticism has fed the beast and created an environment of mistrust and cynicism.

As a teacher and leadership consultant specializing in team leadership and situational leadership, I work with parents, teachers, employees, and managers. By focusing on trust, ownership, and effective team skills I help them build a climate of trust and improve individual and team performance.

However, the importance of this book actually has nothing to do with who I am or what I do. Let me illustrate what I mean.

Have you ever heard of Jim Thorpe?

Jim Thorpe is often described as the greatest athlete of the twentieth century. Jim Thorpe was a world class baseball player, world class track star, and a world class football player. He won several medals at the 1912 World Olympics. He played professional baseball and professional football at the same time. He was definitely a great athlete. Now, let me ask you another question:

Who was Jim Thorpe's coach?

You may have never heard of him. You certainly won't see his name discussed very often outside the sports enthusiast arena. His name was Pop Warner.

Why the question?

It's simple. Pop Warner could not have competed with Jim Thorpe in any event. He couldn't have even come close. However, Pop Warner could bring out the best in Jim Thorpe.

I have spent over 35 years trying to bring the best out of my children, students, employees, and those I have trained. The purpose of this book is to help bring the best out of those who read and practice the principles taught within its pages. The principles in this book are true. They have survived the test of time.

I hope you find the message within this short book meaningful. I know if you practice The Principles of The Rose you will add beauty to the garden around you and make a difference in the world.

Not All Roses Bloom On The Same Day

Prologue

I call myself a learning facilitator. I create interactive learning experiences designed to help people learn principles and improve performance. I have never had a day that I didn't look forward to going to work. I love being a father, teacher, and consultant. My multiple roles have taught me that Alexander Pope was right when he heralded a message of hope in his work entitled, "An Essay on Man" written in 1733:

"Hope springs eternal in the human breast."

I remember the excitement of my first day teaching at Bonneville High School in Idaho Falls, Idaho. I arrived at school at 5 a.m. in an attempt make sure everything was just right. I organized my classroom, perfected my bulletin boards, and reviewed my lesson plan. Just as the bell rang, a student sauntered into the classroom, closing the door behind him. Ten minutes later, no other students had arrived.

I wondered where everyone was. I asked the student who had shown up for class if he knew the whereabouts of his classmates. He told me he thought they were in the hall just outside the classroom. I opened the door only to find my students standing in the hall just outside the door. I asked firmly why they were not in class. They quickly informed me that they could not come into the class because the door was locked.

When I had arrived, I had forgotten to unlock the door and they were locked out of my classroom when the first student closed the door. Yep, hope springs eternal. Thank goodness I would get another shot the next day! That's one of the fortunate opportunities afforded teachers.

A year later, I was getting ready to teach my first course at Snow College, in Utah. I was so excited. It was Introduction to Business; what a fun class to teach. I was nervous. I remember standing outside the door straightening my tie and taking three deep breaths before entering the room. I now had a year of teaching under my belt. I had my Master's Degree in Business.

I felt like a fountain of knowledge and I was about to give my students a drink. I taught the lesson I had prepared. The delivery was perfect, the reception was not so perfect. As I exited the classroom, I was struck by the realization that I might be a fountain of knowledge, but no one was thirsty.

Not All Roses Bloom On The Same Day

Twelve years later, I was teaching at Weber State University, in Utah. I was excited to be working with a mix of traditional and non-traditional students. I was teaching a rather challenging evening course; Sales Engineering. In this course, the students had to work together in teams to complete a very demanding project. I dismissed the students, picked up my notes, and headed for my office in an adjacent building.

As I opened the door and stepped into the building, I saw three students getting up off the floor. A 51-year-old student, their teammate, had literally knocked them to the floor. Why? The three had not carried their weight on the term project. The older student was doing all the work and he'd had enough. The hope I had for these students diminished as I pondered what had just taken place.

A few years later, I was training at a local company. I was working with a company that manufactured metal sinks. The team I was working with was the box team. They worked eight hours a day putting metal sinks in boxes.

As we started the training, the plant manager stood up in front of the team and announced that he wanted them to redesign the box, cut the cost of the box, improve the protection, and reduce the labor cost per sink. Then he left the room.

I can't write what the team members said after the plant manager left the room and still maintain a family-friendly book. Their cursing and complaining went on and on for what seemed like an eternity. All of a sudden, there was dead silence, and they all turned around and looked at me! My hope was wavering at that instant! I knew nothing about boxing metal sinks.

This book is for young and old alike. It is for students, parents, teachers, and leaders who have found themselves in situations that have caused them to feel like giving up, either on themselves or others.

My focus on continuous improvement has led me to a teaching method I love. I call it "interactive facilitation." This methodology allows me to engage students as partners in learning. Using it, students have the opportunity to interact with the subject matter in a way that increases retention. When students interact with principles being taught, learning lasts. My goal is to facilitate a learning experience for my children, students, and employees; an experience that allows them to learn principles and internalize them. Ten years from now, they will remember and will be able to apply the lessons in the various settings in which they may find themselves.

Some of the most important principles in my life I learned in a small garden and around a kitchen table from a very wise grandmother. I have never forgotten the principles she taught. It is my hope that, through this simple story about a grandmother and her grandson, you will learn and remember the "Principles of the Rose." As you read this parable, you will learn the principles and gain the personal power and hope contained in this simple phrase:

"Not All Roses Bloom on the Same Day"

Not All Roses Bloom On The Same Day

Introduction

As a young man in the 1960's growing up in Utah, I spent a great deal of time with my Grandma Dove. I lived with my grandmother through many of my formative years, until I turned nine or ten.

Years later, when I was in the eighth grade we moved just down the street from my Grandma and Grandpa Dove. It was then that I began helping grandma with her rose garden. This continued until my senior year of high school. Every spring, she would ask me to help her prune her roses, clean the garden, fertilize, and water. In the fall, I would help mound the soil around the base of the roses and do a light pruning.

Grandma loved her rose garden. It was the most beautiful in the neighborhood. When it was in full bloom it was, as the neighbors put it, a site to behold. As we worked in the garden together and enjoyed her homemade treats and snacks, I didn't realize that Grandma wasn't just growing roses, she was growing a young man. . .

All Roses Bloom

Based on a story shared by
Rick Dove

Rose pruning at my Grandma's house,
much yard work to be done.
Preparing for the winter time,
Not my idea of fun.

Some roses looking not so bad,
Though worth my attention.
Some roses looking pretty sad,
I had apprehension.

Grandma helped me understand
all had worth, each one.
So side by side, I worked that day,
with Grandma in the sun.

Remembered still, the lesson learned
among those stems and vines.
"You see," she said "All roses bloom,
some bloom at different times."

J.W. Clements

The Pruning

Grasping the hand pruners tightly, I got down on all fours and carefully reached into the rose bush to prune it.

"Ouch!" I cried out in pain.

"Are you okay, Ricky?" Grandma asked. "You'd better be careful, or those thorns will get you," she chuckled.

"You're telling me!" I replied.

At sixteen, I couldn't believe I was on all fours pruning these half dead rose bushes. It seemed like I was pruning in a hornet's nest. It seemed like the older the rose, the bigger the thorns.

"I don't know why you want to grow roses, these thorns are terrible!" I uttered, somewhat disgruntled as I looked at my hands already scratched and bleeding.

Grandma looked down over the top of her glasses, and said, "I know the thorns are bad, but when the roses bloom, it will make up for the pain."

"Do you remember how beautiful they were last year?" Grandma asked.

"Yes Grandma," I nodded in reluctant agreement.

I thought to myself, "Grandma Dove's roses were always beautiful and they were talk of the neighborhood." I still wondered why roses were Grandma's favorite. I thought to myself, "How can anyone love a flower that is covered with thorns and requires so much work?" I kept that thought to myself because I knew there would be no winning the debate with Grandma. Besides, when we were done we would go to Grandma's kitchen and enjoy one of her homemade treats.

"Ricky, you need to prune that rose to your left," Grandma directed.

"Grandma, I don't think pruning that one will help. It looks like its dead," I muttered under my breath. "I really don't think pruning it is going to bring it back, it looks like a bunch of thorny dead sticks."

Grandma looked directly at me over the top of her spectacles and said, "Come on Ricky, just go ahead and prune it. Remember, not all roses bloom on the same day."

I wondered what Grandma was talking about. "What do roses blooming have to do with pruning a dead rose bush?" I thought to myself.

Reluctantly, I stretched the hand pruners into the plant. "Ouch!" Another deep scratch. This one hurt a lot.

Looking at my hand and wincing at the stinging pain, I said, "Grandma, I'm going to need a bandage. I'm bleeding all over."

Patting me on the shoulder, Grandma said in her comforting way, "Come on honey, let's go inside and get one. While we're at it, maybe we can enjoy a snack. I just pulled a couple loaves of bread out of the oven this morning. I think we need a break anyway, don't you?"

I nodded in eager agreement. I thought to myself, "There's nothing better than Grandma's homemade bread and jam. It's better than cake. Besides, my hands are killing me."

"Come in here, Ricky," Grandma said, motioning to the kitchen. She reached into a cupboard, selected a bandage that would work, and carefully placed it on my hand. Then she suggested, "Let's sit down and enjoy some bread and jam."

I watched as she uncovered the freshly baked bread and carefully cut three thick slices of bread. I could smell it already. Grandma carried her tasty treat to the table and sat down beside me.

"Thanks Grandma, it looks great!" I said.

As we sat together at the kitchen table, I looked at the two thick slices of homemade bread in front of me. I spread the fresh butter and strawberry jam on each slice. My mouth was watering as I took my first bite.

With my mouth half full, I said, "This is really good Grandma."

She nodded in agreement. Then she looked across the table at me and asked, "How's school going?"

I felt a little uncomfortable. I knew she was going to ask about school. Unfortunately, it was not going so well. My parents, after seeing my grades over the past two years, had quit asking about them. All they asked now was, "Did you get all your credits?" To make matters even worse, during my year-end counseling interview, the counselor told me that I didn't appear to be college material. All this left me wondering what I was going to do after high school.

Looking down at the bread and jam on my plate and hurriedly swallowing, I replied somewhat hesitantly, "School's going okay . . . I guess."

Grandma, sensing my hesitance, probed a little deeper. "How do you like your teachers?"

I was silent for a moment and answered, "I like most of my teachers, but my math teacher Mr. Burley is a real grouch. He treats us like we're not trying. He talks so fast, none of us can keep up. Then he gets mad when we can't solve the math problems. He is one of the worst teachers I've ever had!" I said, expressing my frustration.

Mr. Burley was a music teacher that had been assigned to teach math. It was obvious he loved music and didn't like math. This didn't help the students at all. When we didn't complete our homework, he would call us out by name and embarrass us. I thought to myself, "I really don't like him!"

"Sounds like a thorny situation," Grandma chuckled a little, looking at the bandage on my hand.

"Since you don't like your math teacher, what do you think you can do?" she asked.

"What do you mean?" I asked somewhat surprised. "I can't do anything. He's just flat out a lousy teacher!"

I wondered, does she really think I should do something? He's the teacher, I'm just the student. There's nothing I can do! I took another bite of bread and jam.

Looking over the top of her spectacles, Grandma asked, "If I remember right, you're graduating next year?"

"Yes Grandma," I replied. "I've earned all my credits. I just completed my annual interview with my counselor. One more year and I'll graduate."

"So, have you thought about going to college?" Grandma continued, "That would really be exciting. You could be the first one in the Dove family to graduate from college."

I looked at her, thinking about the interview with my counselor, and explained, "When I met with the counselor, he asked what I wanted to do after high school. I told him that I wanted to go to college and study to be a dentist. He looked at my grades and said I didn't appear to be college material. Then he told me college isn't for everyone."

"How did that make you feel?" Grandma asked, reaching out and placing her hand on my shoulder.

"Stupid," I uttered as I pulled away in embarrassment. "I have pretty much given up on the idea of going to college. I don't know what I'm going to do."

"Ricky, it seems like you're feeling discouraged," Grandma said.

"Yes, I'm discouraged and I'm angry. Who's the counselor to tell me I'm not college material? My friend Kip went to college and I know my grades are as good as his."

Grandma looked at me and said, "Maybe I can help. I don't enjoy seeing you so angry and bitter. It sounds like you need to hear about the Principles of The Rose."

I looked at Grandma quizzically and said, "I've never heard of any Principles of The Rose, but I don't think how I'm feeling has anything to do with roses."

Grandma replied, "Well maybe I can convince you. You know I like a challenge," Grandma chuckled. "Would you like my help?"

"I guess I can use all the help I can get." I replied.

"Ricky, you've been helping me with the rose garden for three years now. I think you'll be able to understand what I'm going to tell you.

Think about what we do each spring when we work in the rose garden. We always begin with the pruning, just like we did today. Pruning is important. It helps channel the food and water, which helps the plant produce more blossoms."

Not All Roses Bloom On The Same Day

When we pruned the roses today, what was the first thing you noticed?" Grandma asked.

That's easy," I responded, wrinkling my brow as I looked at my hands, "the thorns!"

"You're right, the thorns," Grandma laughed.

"Ricky, the closer we get to the rose, the easier it is to focus on the thorns. Sometimes we lose sight of how beautiful the rose will be because the blossoms are a hope and the thorns a reality. Even when the roses are in full bloom, the thorns are still there. However, when we focus on the rose, the beauty of the rose dwarfs the thorns."

"Ricky, people are a lot like roses. They are beautiful, however, each has their own set of thorns. The thorns can cause us to lose sight of the good in our teachers, friends, and loved ones. When we become too focused on the thorns, we fail to see the rose.

Sometimes we look at ourselves and only see the thorns. It can be discouraging and can keep us from seeing the beauty of the rose within. Sometimes we may even give up on ourselves. You need to remember the First Principle of The Rose.

One of the greatest strengths a person can have is the ability to see past the thorns and see the rose within.

I thought for a moment about what Grandma was saying. "Was she right? Was it my responsibility to see the good in a grouchy old math teacher? What about my counselor?" I wasn't sure I liked the First Principle of The Rose. I asked myself, "Can there really be good in everyone?"

As I stood up and headed to the door, I looked at Grandma and asked, "Is there more to the Principles of The Rose? I need to hear more, I'm not sure I understand."

Pausing for a moment Grandma responded, "Yes, Ricky. When you come tomorrow, I will share the Second Principle of the Rose. For now, just consider what we've talked about today."

"Okay, see you tomorrow Grandma," I waved goodbye as I hurried home.

One of the greatest strengths a person can have is the ability to see past the thorns and see the rose within.

Not All Roses Bloom On The Same Day

Reflection

Fifty years later, as I reflect on my conversations with Grandma I am reminded that in my annual interview with my counselor I was asked what I wanted to do after graduation. I told my counselor that I'd like to go to college and study to be a dentist. The counselor looked at my file and said, "Ricky, your grades don't indicate that you would be successful in college. You know college isn't for everyone."

I was shattered. What my counselor didn't know was that for the last six months I had been reading books from the library on chemistry, zoology, biology, and math. As I read the books, I would memorize the terms and formulas. During this six months, my confidence and my grades had been gradually improving, even though I was working about 20 to 30 hours a week bagging groceries at a local market.

I joined the National Guard during my senior year of high school. Upon graduation, I entered basic training at Fort Leonard Wood, Missouri, then I worked for the next year in my father's retail grocery business. When I turned 19, I began a two year mission in Norway for the Church of Jesus Christ of Latter-day Saints.

Upon my return, I attended Snow College in Utah. I met my wife Mary, and we were married in 1974. I graduated from Snow College and attended Utah State University, graduating at the top of my class at Utah State.

I must admit, there have been times I would have liked to have spoken with my high school counselor again. However, I realize now that I allowed the rose within me to be hidden by my thorns, and the counselor had no way of knowing what I was doing on my own.

It is important to allow others to see the rose within.

The Cleaning

I was up early the next day. I couldn't stop thinking about the First Principle of The Rose. I thought to myself, "I understand what Grandma's saying, but it's just not that easy to ignore the thorns in others. At least it's not as easy as Grandma makes it sound. Mr. Burley is a real grouch. If he has a rose inside, he keeps it well hidden."

I glanced at the clock and headed out the door to Grandma's house. I wanted to start cleaning the garden early. Grandma's rose garden was exposed to full sunlight after 9. She was always saying, "Sunlight is important for growing roses."

Knocking on Grandma's door and stepping into the house, I called out from the entryway, "Grandma, I'm here!"

"Come on in, Ricky," she called from the kitchen, "I'm just pulling a couple of pies out of the oven."

"I love Grandma's pies," I thought to myself, my mouth already watering.

As I entered the kitchen, Grandma looked up as she carefully placed the freshly baked pies on the cooling tray and asked, "Are you ready to get started?"

"You bet, Grandma. I was thinking we should get started before it gets too hot."

"Good thinking Ricky, it can get awfully warm. Let's get it done, then we can come inside and enjoy a slice of pie." Grandma stood by the pies and while looking over at me. She took a big whiff and jokingly asked, "Would you like a piece of pie when we're done?"

"You bet I would, Grandma!" I replied, grinning from ear to ear as we headed outside.

On our way to the garden, we stopped at the shed to get the rakes and hoes we would need to clean the garden.

Grandma opened the shed door. While scanning the assortment of tools, she said, "You know Ricky, it is important to use the right tools to clean the garden. If we don't use the right tools, we won't be able to clean the garden without damaging the roses."

Grandma carefully selected the hoes and rakes we would need, shut the shed door, and we headed for the garden.

As we began cleaning the garden, I looked over at Grandma and said, "I've been thinking about what you said yesterday. I would like to see the good in others, but it's really hard to find in some people.

You know, like Mr. Burley. I'm sure it's easy for you. It seems like you're always able to see the good in others. I have a hard time with it. I really don't know how to begin."

"Well Ricky," Grandma replied, "It's always good to begin at the beginning."

"What do you mean?" I asked.

Grandma stood up, took a deep breath, wiped a bead of sweat from her brow with her handkerchief, and continued. "It's really quite simple Ricky: begin with yourself."

Leaning on her hoe, Grandma looked across the garden at me and said, "Think about our conversation yesterday. You indicated you were discouraged. You said your grades were not what you wanted them to be. You also said you were angry with your counselor who suggested you weren't college material. You seemed to be saying you had given up going to college."

"I remember," I said, looking down at my feet, and shaking my head. "I was feeling discouraged, and sorry for myself. The whole thing made me feel hurt and angry at the same time."

"I know Ricky," Grandma said stepping closer and placing her hand on my shoulder. "When someone focuses on your thorns and then goes the extra mile to point them out, it hurts."

"That's why you always begin with yourself," Grandma continued. "When you have people pointing out your weaknesses, you may feel discouraged, hurt, angry, frustrated, or even vengeful. These kinds of feelings can cause you to lose confidence. When you lose your confidence, you won't feel good about yourself. It's almost impossible to find success if you don't feel good about yourself."

"That's exactly what I've been feeling," I added. "I really don't feel good about myself. I was actually embarrassed to tell you. I want you, Mom, and Dad to be proud of me."

"Ricky, I hope you know your parents and I love you very much," Grandma said. "We are very proud of you. You're a fine young man. Just look at how much you've helped me in the garden."

"Grandma, I enjoy helping you. I want to be successful. I want to feel like I can make a difference."

Grandma looked over the top of her spectacles and asked, "Do you understand what we are doing in the garden today?"

"Yes Grandma," I replied. "We're cleaning it. We're getting rid of all the leaves and junk."

"Exactly!" Grandma affirmed.

Then she asked, "Why do you think cleaning the garden is so important?"

"I'm not sure, but I guess when we get rid of all this junk it helps the roses grow."

"You're right!" Grandma said. "We're getting rid of all the junk. All the clutter that will keep the roses from growing to their potential.

"Listen closely. You told me you would like to be successful and you'd like to make a difference. That being the case, you need to remove the junk."

"What do you mean by junk?" I asked.

She explained, "Junk is anything that chokes our potential. Think of it as clutter. You see the rose within us can never bloom if it can't get what it needs. We can't give it what it needs if we can't see through the clutter."

"I think I understand. You're saying I need to get rid of anything holding me back," I paraphrased.

"Yes Ricky," Grandma replied. "When we remove this clutter from the garden, the roses get more water and more nourishment, grow stronger, and produce more beautiful blooms. When you remove the negative thoughts, attitudes, and habits that are holding you back, the rose within you will grow and begin to reveal itself. It's then, and only then, that you'll feel good about yourself and be able to make a difference."

"Grandma, how do I remove my thorns?" I asked. "I can't just make them go away."

Grandma looked up and replied, "No Ricky, you can't just make them disappear. Remember, a rose will always have its thorns. They are a part of the rose. However, ask yourself this: Once the rose blooms, do we focus on the rose or the thorns?"

"The rose of course," I replied.

Resting her hand on my shoulder Grandma continued, "Ricky, it's all about what you focus on; the rose or the thorns. Some of our thorns will be with us our entire lives, but we don't have to let them control us. Use the right tools to clear the clutter so you can stay focused on the rose. Do you understand what I am trying to say?"

Grandma wiped her forehead with her handkerchief and resumed cleaning the garden.

"I think I understand, Grandma. The Principles of The Rose are meant to help me improve myself. But you keep saying use the right tools. What are the right tools?"

"Ricky, the right tool is anything that helps remove the clutter and grows the rose within. For example, you mentioned you were reading books to help you learn science. You also mentioned your grades have been improving. Those books are tools, and apparently the right ones. Sometimes we find the tools and sometimes others help us find them. Either way, the right tools help us clear away the clutter and enable us to focus on the rose."

I shoveled the piles of debris we had removed from the garden into a trash can. Looking over the rose garden, I realized we had finished cleaning it. I could not believe how fast the morning had gone.

"Wow, it looks like we're done, Grandma!" I said.

"I believe we are," Grandma replied.

Not All Roses Bloom On The Same Day

Lowering her spectacles and winking at me, Grandma asked, "Do you still have time for a piece of pie?"

"You better believe it!" I laughed.

We quickly cleaned the rakes and hoes and put them back in the shed. I turned to Grandma, thanked her for her help, and gave her a hug. Then we headed into the house.

Once inside, I sat down at the kitchen table. Grandma cut two huge pieces of apple pie and set the table with the pie and two glasses of ice cold milk. I took a bite of pie and washed it down with a drink of milk.

"This is really good, Grandma," I said as I took another bite.

"I'm glad you like it. You know there's more where that came from," Grandma said, gesturing toward the two large pies on the cooling trays.

"Tell me Ricky, did you learn anything today?" Grandma asked.

"Yes Grandma, I did. I learned that to follow the Principles of The Rose, I need to begin at the beginning, so I should begin with myself."

"Good!" Grandma interjected.

"I also learned that I need to figure out what's holding me back and try to remove it. Then I should focus on the rose within me. This will help me to feel better about myself."

"That's right," Grandma said.

Grandma continued, "Ricky, sometimes it is hard to get rid of the things that hold us back. It's important to have a willingness to change and the courage to move forward with faith in ourselves. Always focus with faith on the rose within. You need to remember the Second Principle of The Rose."

Begin with yourself, clear away the clutter, and focus with faith on the rose within.

"Well you made quick work of that pie," Grandma quipped. "Can you come next Saturday and help me in the garden again?"

"Sure Grandma!" I replied. "What are we going to do?"

"I think next week we'll feed the roses," Grandma answered.

Grandma tipped her spectacles a little lower so as to look right into my eyes and said, "Next week I will teach you the Third Principle of The Rose."

"Thanks for the pie, Grandma, and the lesson. I'll always remember what you've taught me. See you Saturday."

On the way home, I thought about everything my grandmother had taught me that day. I thought about some of the clutter that might be holding me back. I wasn't sure how I was going to clear it.

I thought about grouchy Mr. Burley and my counselor. I also thought about the negative attitude I was developing. I wasn't even sure what tools I needed to fix these problems. However, I knew I wanted to change my focus and be better so I could make a difference.

Begin with yourself, clear away the clutter, and focus with faith on the rose within.

Reflection

A s I ponder the message of the cleaning, I look back on the choices I made as a young man and the impact those decisions had on my life. It is very clear now, but it was not so clear when I was making those decisions.

It takes time to connect to the tools that can help you clear your personal clutter. I guess that is one reason Grandma always reminded me "not all roses bloom on the same day." I come from a family background filled with all kinds of clutter. It may be one reason I spent so much time with my grandmother.

I had loving parents, and I loved them very much. I knew they loved me. However, they seemed to have a hard time getting along with each other. Over the course of several years, they were divorced once and separated more than once. I didn't come from the most stable of home environments. I think my parents loved each other in their own way, they simply had a hard time showing it.

I came to understand that my sense of security or lack of security was affected by the constant turmoil in our family. When I had a sense of belonging in my family, I had a strong sense of security. However, when my parents were separated or divorced, I felt a lack of belonging and a total lack of security. When my parents got back together, my sense of belonging and security returned.

I believe that the desire to belong is one of the most powerful influences on human behavior. It may be the most powerful. A person can belong in a positive way or in a negative way. I was fortunate to find a way to belong in a positive way in my family and with my Grandma.

As I began my military training at Fort Leonard Wood, Missouri, I truly thought that I had died and gone to hell. They shaved me bald, gave me shots, and I was being called names I had never heard before. The army put me through training that was more grueling than I could have ever imagined.

One day during a little exercise called "tree drill", our entire platoon was ordered to climb a 20-foot tree. I was doing pretty well until someone above me stepped on my hand and I fell from the top of the tree, dislocating my knee.

Not All Roses Bloom On The Same Day

When I arrived at the hospital, they put a full-length cast on my leg. The same day another young man broke his foot and had to have a cast as well. Typically we would have been transferred to a reception center until we were healthy, then we would have started basic training over again. This was called recycling. However, neither of us wanted to start over, having already gone through the first three weeks of basic training.

We heard through the grapevine that the "tree drill" was strictly prohibited. Our sergeants could have been in deep trouble for forcing the platoon to climb that tree. They didn't want any of their superiors to find out about our injuries. They decided it would be better if we stayed with our unit and didn't recycle. For us, that meant following the platoon on crutches for the next seven weeks while completing our basic training. You haven't lived until you have walked five miles or more on crutches. I don't recommend it.

When it came time to go to the firing range, I was worried. We had to shoot from a fox hole in a sitting position. This meant I would have to come up with a way to jump into the fox hole and shoot from a sitting position with a full-length cast on my leg.

We practiced daily for about two weeks, and my backside was sore because in order to sit, I had to swing my leg with the cast forward and just fall on my backside. It was painful, but effective.

Not All Roses Bloom On The Same Day

We all had to pass the firing range test at the end of the two weeks. My friend who broke his foot and I shot at expert level during the test, so we earned a three-day pass. We decided to visit the Lake of the Ozarks. We were quite a sight laying in our beds, in the cabin, with our legs propped up on pillows, but it was better than being back at Fort Leonard Wood.

My military experience taught me discipline. It taught me how to push myself beyond what I thought was possible and how to have faith to overcome obstacles. All these tools served me well in clearing away some of the clutter holding me back. I completed my training successfully and returned home to prepare for a two-year LDS mission.

My mission to Norway was another milestone in my life. Because of my military experience, I had some of the tools I needed to serve a successful mission. While in Norway, I learned to love the Norwegian people. They were not all that interested in our gospel message, but they were happy, fun-loving, and kind. I loved my two years in Norway.

On the spiritual side of my life, I strengthened my faith and gained the ability to love unconditionally. I developed my people skills and learned how to study - both very necessary when you are trying to learn a new language. I will be forever grateful to the Norwegian people for the kindness they showed me during my two years there.

I attended Snow College after my mission. It was there that I met and married my sweet wife, Mary. Our union was like "A Tale of Two Cities." Her family was very strong. She had developed tremendous faith and the ability to love. As I looked in her eyes, I thought to myself *I will never love more than this.* The day we were married was the greatest day of my life, and it changed my life forever.

While I completed my college degrees, we had our first two children, Kenny and Amy. When I held each of them for the first time, my love expanded. We had our third child, Rikki, my namesake, a little over a year after I graduated, and my ability to love grew even more, but we were not done growing our family.

Our next three children, Cami, Michael, and Kirsten were born, and our love grew with the birth of each one. I could write volumes on each of my children and what they have taught me. However, I would like to share a short story about one of them.

Our daughter Cami was born with developmental disabilities. We didn't know at first. However, as she was delayed in reaching the normal milestones like sitting, crawling, and walking, we began to suspect something might be wrong.

When she started walking, she would try to walk through a doorway and walk into the corner of the door frame. A friend observed this one evening and suggested we have her tested. After many tests, we determined that she had a cognitive disability. We put her in preschool. It helped, but she needed more.

Mary arranged for an occupational therapist to come to our home and work with her. I remember Mary helping her learn her letters using string licorice. She could see and feel the letters. When she identified the letter correctly, she got to eat the licorice. I am sure there are many who can relate to this challenge.

Before Cami was born, I worried about having a child with disabilities. I had always felt it would be very hard to have a child with these challenges. I had done a lot of work with Muscular Dystrophy Association (MDA) and I got to see firsthand what the parents did for their children. I thought they were making a tremendous sacrifice. I guess I thought the extra work would cut into the love. I couldn't have been more wrong.

When we discovered Cami's disabilities, we did everything we could to identify and help her overcome her challenges. Watching her undergo the medical and mental testing was extremely painful for Mary and me.

Cami, however, has proven to be a blessing in our lives. She has helped Mary and me to develop an even greater ability to love, and taught us how to love unconditionally.

Not All Roses Bloom On The Same Day

We have watched Cami grow into a beautiful young woman. Her faith knows no bounds. She works very hard to overcome obstacles. Her optimism is inspiring. Through the years, many of her friends have moved on and out of her life. It hurts her, of course, but she has the resilience to rise to the challenge and make new friends.

Cami is easy to love, and she loves everyone without guile. Aunt Cami is special to each of her nieces and nephews. At age thirty, Cami is a living example of the message "Not All Roses Bloom on the Same Day." I would like to add, "But all Roses Bloom."

Did you know that some experts believe that roses can live forever when properly cared for? People have the same potential. We simply need to find out where they are, meet them there, and provide for them what they can't provide for themselves.

Mary and I now have six children, five of whom are married. We also have 13 beautiful grandchildren. Our love has expanded in unexplainable ways. It has helped me clear the clutter so my life could bloom. What have I learned?

Faith, love, and patience are three of the most important tools you need to clean your garden and develop the rose within.

Faith, love, and patience are three of the most important tools you need to clean your garden and develop the rose within.

The Feeding

The next day was Sunday. I spent the entire day thinking about everything Grandma had said. I wondered what I could do that might help me have a better attitude.

As I was lying in bed Sunday evening, I was struck by a simple thought. I had never really spoken directly to Mr. Burley about the problems I was having in the math class. I realized I had always just blamed my poor math scores on Mr. Burley. I decided I would talk to Mr. Burley first thing Monday morning and ask him for some suggestions. "Could the solution really be that simple?"

I was up early the next morning. I ate a quick breakfast and spent some time finishing an English assignment. I waved goodbye to my mother and ran to the corner to catch the bus.

Once on the bus, I sat quietly rehearsing in my mind what I was going to say to Mr. Burley. I was nervous about talking to him. "I don't think I'd better tell Mr. Burley how grouchy I think he is," I chuckled to myself.

I wasn't sure how to begin.

"Maybe I should just tell him I'm struggling because I can't keep up with his lectures."

"I don't know what I'm going to say. This whole thing is probably a bad idea," I thought to myself with some frustration. I decided just to play it by ear.

As I approached Mr. Burley's classroom, I cautiously peeked around the corner of the door to see if he was in his room. I saw him sitting at his desk in the corner correcting assignments. I had never seen a pen move so fast.

"Mr. Burley better slow down or he's going to run out of ink," I chuckled. I took a deep breath and entered the room.

"Mr. Burley, am I interrupting you?" I asked, somewhat cautiously.

"Come in Mr. Dove, I was just finishing some grading, but I have a few minutes," Mr. Burley replied in his deep, husky voice.

Actually, Mr. Burley's voice always sounded a little hoarse. This was almost funny because Mr. Burley had once been a music teacher. The joke at school was that he had lost his singing voice and that was why the principal moved him from teaching music to teaching math. It probably was not true, but it made a good story.

"What can I do for you Mr. Dove?" Mr. Burley asked.

"Mr. Burley, I really need your help. I'm struggling in math. I've tried to pay attention to your lectures, but I have a hard time keeping up. I'm not doing well on the assignments and tests. I'd like get higher scores. Do you have any suggestions on how I can do better? "

Mr. Burley looked at me, put his pen down, leaned back in his chair, and clasped his hands behind his head.

"Mr. Dove, sit down for a minute," he directed me with his eyes to the chair at the side of his desk. "Let me ask you a couple of questions."

"First, are you asking questions in class?"

"Yes Mr. Burley," I replied. "At least when there is time to ask questions."

Mr. Burley smiled and said, "Good. I appreciate it when students speak up in class and ask questions."

Then he asked, "Are you spending one to two hours a night working on math?"

"Well, probably not every night. When I work on math, I usually spend at least an hour," I answered. "I probably work on math about four nights a week."

"Well, not perfect, but not bad!" Mr. Burley nodded in approval.

He glanced at the clock and asked, "Could you come in right after school?"

"Right now I am scheduled to work right after school," I replied, "but I could call and arrange to go in later."

Mr. Burley clarified, "If you can reschedule, I have a study group that I work with for about an hour after school each day. It gives me a chance to answer all the questions in a slower-paced session."

"Really!" I responded, somewhat taken back. "You really spend an hour after school each day helping students?" I asked.

"You sound surprised, Mr. Dove!" Mr. Burley said with a smile on his face. "Are you telling me you didn't think this old grouch would do something like that?

Struggling to find the right words, I replied, "No I... just ..."

"You didn't think I knew you thought I was grouchy, did you?" Mr. Burley asked while looking me straight in the eye.

At first I wondered if Grandma had called him, but I quickly brushed the idea aside. That just wasn't her style.

"I'm really sorry," I apologized, looking down.

"How did you know?" I asked, somewhat embarrassed.

"I'm old, Mr. Dove, not deaf!" Mr. Burley responded.

He started laughing. Between his big, deep belly laughs he said, "Mr. Dove, don't worry. I don't expect perfection, just honest effort. I announced the extra help session in class, but you must have missed it."

Mr. Burley continued, "You see, I have to teach students who would get bored if I went slower, while at the same time, I have to help students who are not quite as up to speed on math. The only free time I have to help the students who are struggling is after school. That is why I've always held extra help sessions after school."

He leaned back in his chair, again smiling proudly. "Yes Mr. Dove, I've been doing the extra help sessions for about ten years now."

"Can I still attend the help session?" I asked.

"Sure, I'd love to have you there," Mr. Burley said.

"I'll be there today!" I said emphatically.

"I'll look forward to it," he said with a friendly smile.

The first bell rang, signaling that it was time to go to class. I thanked Mr. Burley and stood up to leave. As I was leaving, I turned back.

Clearing my throat a little, I said, "I want to apologize again, Mr. Burley. Thanks for listening."

He smiled as he returned to his grading. Without looking up, he said, "No problem Mr. Dove. I'll see you later today."

I headed to first period with a smile on my face. I thought to myself, "How could I have been so wrong about Mr. Burley?"

"Grandma was right," I thought. "When we ignore the thorns and focus on the rose, good things happen. Even grouchy old Mr. Burley has a rose inside." As I entered my first period class, I thought, "I can't believe how much better I feel."

I attended the after-school sessions for the rest of the week. On Friday, I passed the test with my highest score of the term. I came to realize that Mr. Burley was actually a good teacher.

Early Saturday morning, I literally jumped out of bed. I was excited to tell Grandma about my week. She would be happy to hear I was trying to use the principles she had taught me. I was pleased myself.

As I walked up the driveway, I could see Grandma in the back yard. She waved when she saw me.

With a smile on my face, I waved back, "Good morning, Grandma!"

"Good morning," she replied, "You seem to be in an extra good mood today. What's with that big smile?"

"I'm excited to tell you what happened at school this week!"

"Did you meet a cute girl?" Grandma teased.

"No nothing like that," I replied shyly.

"I talked to Mr. Burley this week about the problems I've been having in his math class."

"How did it go?" Grandma asked half smiling. "Did you tell him you thought he was a grouch?"

"No, I didn't have to tell him. I'm not sure how, but he already knew," I replied.

"Actually, our talk went really well, I couldn't believe it," I said. "He actually holds an hour study session every day after school. I didn't realize how much extra time Mr. Burley spends with his students. He really isn't grouchy at all. Once you get to know him, he's really nice."

Lowering her spectacles and looking me in the eye, Grandma asked, "So he isn't quite the lousy teacher you thought he was?"

"No Grandma," I said somewhat embarrassed. "I was really wrong. I felt terrible and I apologized."

"Grandma, you were right! Everyone does have a rose inside. You just have to make an effort to find it."

"I am proud of you, Ricky," Grandma said, patting me lovingly on the shoulder. "It takes a big person to admit they were wrong. It seems you are beginning to understand the first two Principles of The Rose. I think you're ready for the third principle. Maybe we can visit while we feed and water the roses."

"When we're done with the garden, are you up for some fresh baked raisin-filled cookies?" Grandma asked.

"You bet I am!" I answered enthusiastically. "Grandma makes the best raisin-filled cookies on the planet," I thought to myself.

"I have mixed the plant food in a mixture of loam," Grandma said. "We'll spread the mixture in a thin layer over the rose bed and then we'll water it. The added food will give the roses a real jump start over the next few weeks."

Grandma continued, "You know Ricky, these roses really need this extra feeding. They can't get enough nutrition on their own. They depend on us to provide it for them."

"How do you know what the roses need Grandma?" I asked.

"Well, for one thing, I have raised roses for decades," Grandma chuckled. "You know I'm older than dirt." "However, I also like to talk to the owner of the nursery where I buy the plant food and loam. He lets me know what he has learned that might help me better care for the roses."

"By the way, did you know experts believe roses can live forever if they are properly cared for?" Grandma added.

"Last but not least, the roses let me know when they begin to grow and thrive. When they begin to bud and bloom, I know I have provided them with what they need. So see, it is really quite simple, isn't it?" Grandma asked with her usual loving, soft smile.

"You make it sound easy," I said. "Everyone says you grow the most beautiful roses in the neighborhood."

Grandma glanced at me and said, "You know, people are a lot like these roses. Sometimes people need things they can't provide for themselves. Sometimes they just can't see what they need. They sort of have a blind spot.

"Therefore, it's important for others around them to help them with what they need, encourage them, and provide for them what they can't provide for themselves. It is kind of like feeding and watering people to help them grow."

"How do you know what people need, Grandma?" I asked.

"They will tell you what they need, if you listen," Grandma replied.

She continued, "People will tell you what they need. However, sometimes you need to ask. It is important to trust them, give them space and time to grow, and always listen. The good Lord gave you two ears and one mouth, and you should use them proportionately. Trust me, people will tell you what they need."

"That is sort of what I did when I talked to Mr. Burley," I added. "I needed his help and I needed to learn at a slower pace. I would have never known about the after-school help sessions if I hadn't gone to him and told him what I needed. Not only that, I got to see a whole new side of Mr. Burley."

"Exactly," Grandma said, placing her hand on my shoulder. "Always trust the goodness in people. Very few people go through life trying to make this world a more miserable place to live."

Grandma stood up, looked around the rose garden, and smiled. "It looks like we're done Ricky. Let's put the water on the garden and then we can go enjoy some of those cookies," she said winking at me.

It wasn't long before Grandma and I were sitting at the kitchen table, visiting and joking and enjoying the cookies.

Just as we were finishing our snack, Grandma asked, "Are you ready to learn the Third Principle of the Rose?

"Yes Grandma," I replied. I had been waiting all week to learn it.

Grandma proceeded, "The third principle is directly related to what we did in the garden today. I think this will make sense given what we've talked about.

We all need others to provide for us what we cannot provide for ourselves."

She continued, "None of us gets through this life alone. We've all had parents, teachers, or leaders who provided for us what we were not prepared to provide for ourselves."

"Yes Grandma," I added, "that's what Mr. Burley did for me."

"Exactly," Grandma said.

"Ricky, we should see blossoms in June," Grandma said, looking at me over the top of her spectacles. "When the roses start to bloom, I will finish teaching you about the Principles of the Rose."

"Why do I have to wait for the roses to start blooming?" I asked.

Placing her hand gently on my shoulder, Grandma replied, "Good things come to those who wait, and patience will help remove the clutter."

I was a little baffled as to how waiting would help clear the clutter, but I trusted Grandma. I gave her a big hug and snatched another cookie on my way out the door.

"Thanks Grandma, love you."

The success I was experiencing with the Principles of The Rose made me feel good about myself. Grandma helped me to be more positive. Without Grandma's help, I'd still be struggling in math and I'd still be angry and discouraged.

With my new-found change in attitude, I felt good about myself and I felt that someday I might be able to make a difference. I would have to wait to learn the rest of the Principles of The Rose, but I was certain it would be worth waiting for.

We all need others to provide for us what we cannot provide for ourselves.

Reflection

As I consider what Grandma taught me during the feeding, I recall my first teaching assignment at Bonneville High School in Idaho Falls. I was assigned to teach a group of students I affectionately refer to as the 'sweat hogs' of Bonneville High School.

I had picked up the term 'sweat hogs' from a popular TV show in the 1970's entitled "Welcome Back Kotter." My students did not want to be in school. As a matter of fact, it seemed at times, the administration didn't want them in school. I taught the students in three separate classes before lunch. After lunch, they would go to work, thus the description 'sweat hogs.' In the afternoon, I would visit them on their job sites. It was my responsibility to keep them employed.

At first, the students didn't seem very motivated. There seemed to be no sense of belonging, in terms of high school. Their sense of belonging came from other sources not related to school. Some of them had real challenges like broken homes, drinking, drugs, and other issues. At first, I wasn't sure what I'd gotten myself into. I really wasn't trained to deal with all of the problems.

As I pondered what I could do to help these students, I decided that I would talk to them about starting a DECA chapter. DECA or Distributive Education Clubs of America is an organization designed for students who study marketing. Of course our class was not designed to study marketing. We focused on learning skills for work.

When I first explained to them what DECA was all about, they were not sure if they wanted to participate. They really didn't know anything about DECA or marketing. I suggested to them that we could attend the Western Regional Conference to be held in Boise, Idaho. In Boise, they could learn about DECA, what membership entailed, and meet other students in the organization. They were all in for a trip to Boise.

I had a very supportive principal who paid the bulk of the cost for 30 students to attend. They attended the conference sessions and had a lot of fun for the next two days. At the end of the conference, they were all excited about DECA. They were especially interested in the state competition that would be held in Moscow, Idaho, later in the school year.

The only problem we had was that we didn't study marketing in our class, so they were not sure how they could compete or what events they could compete in. I suggested we do a chapter competition. At the time it was known as the Muscular Dystrophy event. In this event, the chapter would come up with an idea to raise money for MDA. Then they would go through all of the planning steps: setting goals, assigning roles to each member, organizing, promoting, and raising money for Muscular Dystrophy.

They were really excited about this competition. They asked me if they could sponsor a ski-a-thon. I told them that a ski-a-thon would be great. We had our first planning meeting, and one of the first steps was to set our goals. I would love to tell you that their first goal was to raise money for MDA, however it was actually to get as many students as possible out of school for the ski-a-thon. Their secondary goal was to raise money for Muscular Dystrophy.

They planned and organized the activity. They arranged for prizes for the students who raised the most money in pledges. They were able to get businesses to donate prizes. One of the sporting goods stores donated a set of skis, boots, and poles. They got permission to hold the ski-a-thon on a school day, and we had five buses that took students to the resort.

They were able to raise close to three thousand dollars for Muscular Dystrophy. I will never forget standing on the steps of the high school with a giant check, all of it raised by this ragtag group of students who, when they started, knew nothing about marketing or DECA. The TV station was there as we presented the check to the representative for the Muscular Dystrophy Association. Standing behind me were my 'sweat hogs,' making various gestures over my head in view of the camera.

We took this fundraising project to the state competition and won first place in the state of Idaho. This allowed us to take nine students to Nationals in Houston, Texas.

To offset the costs of the trip to nationals, the students opened a school store. They created it by renovating an oversized janitor's closet. They painted the walls the school colors and put cork board on the top third of the walls for displays. A company donated a cash register and a refrigerator and some shelving. They rented display space on the walls and sold candy, snacks, and drinks before school, at lunch, and after school. They were able to raise thousands of dollars to help offset the cost of going to nationals with enough left over for books for the next year. We attended nationals in Houston, Texas, where they placed in the top ten in the MDA event.

I only had the opportunity of working with these high school students for one year. However, the 'Principles of The Rose' that my grandmother taught me helped me to see the potential in them. I was able to provide for them what they could not provide for themselves, and they experienced success.

Years later, the majority of these students have gone on to successful careers, marriages, and families. They taught me more than I taught them. What did I learn from this experience?

Discover what people need, and provide for them what they cannot provide for themselves.

We all need others to provide for us what we cannot provide for ourselves.

The Blooming

I continued to practice the 'Principles of The Rose.' I was doing better in math, and I actually liked Mr. Burley. I even stopped by the counseling office and spoke to my counselor, who gave me some information on two-year colleges that would accept students with a lower GPA.

I was grateful that Grandma had taught me the first three Principles of The Rose. They had made my life better. Because of the success I was having at school, I really wanted to learn more about the 'Principles of The Rose.' I was growing impatient. I kept asking Grandma to tell me more about the next principle, but she just kept saying I needed to wait.

She would just smile and say, "Ricky, you need to be patient. The roses will bloom in their own time. Just think how beautiful the garden will be when the roses bloom."

It was Saturday. I was out of bed early and ate a quick breakfast, then decided to visit Grandma. I was hoping the roses had bloomed and Grandma would teach me more about the Principles of The Rose.

Not All Roses Bloom On The Same Day

As I entered Grandma's house, I could hear her in the kitchen. She was just finishing up the dishes.

I could smell something baking. "How are you doing this morning Grandma?"

"Pretty good for the shape I'm in," Grandma replied, standing up and stretching her back.

Then with a smile on her face she said, "I've got something to show you."

"Have the roses bloomed?" I asked impatiently.

Grandma smiled and said, "Well, let's go out and take a look,"

"Oh come on Grandma, just tell me," I coaxed.

She didn't answer, she just headed out the door. I followed close behind.

As we approached the garden, I could see several roses in full bloom. There were also roses just starting to bloom as well as some large buds with a hint of color.

I looked at the garden, admiring the blossoms. "They're perfect Grandma."

"Yes they are," Grandma agreed.

Grandma looked at me and asked, "Ricky, when you look at the garden what do you see?"

"Well, I see a few blossoms and a lot of buds. A few of the buds look like they're ready to bloom."

"Anything else?" Grandma asked.

I looked closer. "I can see that half dead rose bush you made me prune a few weeks ago. It has grown, but there's not much happening," I chuckled.

As I examined the rose garden more closely, I noticed that some of the rose bushes were not budding. "Why are they so far behind?" I asked.

Grandma looked at me and placed her hand on my shoulder. "Have you forgotten? Not all roses bloom on the same day."

Then she said, "You can't expect the rose bush that was dying to bloom at the same time as the others. It went through a hard winter and got off to a slow start. We had to prune it back to almost nothing. Give it time; it will catch up. You may find that it ends up producing the most beautiful roses in the garden."

Grandma continued, "That half dead rose bush may not have grown as fast as you would have liked, but look how far it's come."

"Ricky, do you think it's important to recognize progress?"

"I suppose so," I answered tentatively.

Grandma continued, "People are a lot like roses. We need to recognize their progress and show appreciation for the good they do. If we only recognize perfection in ourselves and others, we will be sadly disappointed."

She explained further, "You asked why some of the roses have not bloomed. It may be because some of them are not getting enough light or water."

"That makes sense," I said, nodding in agreement. "I can see some of the shorter roses are shaded by the taller rose bushes."

"I believe you're right," Grandma said. "Some roses may capture most of the light, but that doesn't mean the smaller bushes won't ultimately produce beautiful roses. Just like people, each one will develop in their own time."

"I told you I would finish teaching you about the Principles of The Rose when the roses started to bloom," Grandma said. "First let's go over what we've talked about already."

She looked at me and said, "Listen closely and make sure I don't miss anything. You know I'm getting older. My memory is not as good as it used to be."

First: *One of the greatest strengths a person can have is the ability to see past the thorns and see the rose within.*

Second: *Begin with yourself, clear away the clutter, and focus with faith on the rose within.*

Third: *We all need others to provide for us what we cannot provide for ourselves.*

"Is that about right?" Grandma asked.

"Yes Grandma," I replied.

"Now, let me teach you the Fourth Principle of The Rose."

I had been looking forward to this final lesson. Grandma had helped me so much by teaching me the first three principles that I was anxious to learn the fourth principle.

"Ricky, it takes patience to grow a beautiful rose," Grandma explained. "We must learn what each plant needs. People are just like these rose bushes. They all have different strengths and weaknesses and therefore different needs. If we have patience, and encourage them, and look for an opportunity to help them grow, each person will produce a beautiful rose."

"Ricky, how did you feel when you saw the new rose blossoms this morning?" Grandma asked.

"I felt good." Then I went on to explain, "I've been watching the garden for weeks, and I was beginning to wonder if the roses would ever bloom. We worked hard on the garden, and now it kind of feels like we're being rewarded for our hard work."

"That's right," Grandma said. "It feels good to have had a part in growing something so beautiful. I agree we worked hard on the garden," Grandma said.

"However, we need to remember, the rose did most of the work. If the rose didn't do its part, no matter how hard we worked, it would never bloom. Because the rose does most of the work, it is important to show our appreciation. Some roses are large and beautiful, some roses are small and beautiful."

Each rose, no matter what color, size, or shape, makes a difference and adds beauty to the garden.

Grandma continued, "I have always said: People are like roses, they come in all shapes and sizes."

We need to show love and appreciation to everyone, regardless of color, type, or size. Every person adds beauty to this world and makes a difference.

When we focus on the potential and the good in others and we provide for them what they cannot provide for themselves, we will understand the Fourth Principle of The Rose.

The greatest joy you will ever experience is reaching out and lifting others to new heights.

Looking over her spectacles and placing her hand on my arm Grandma added,

"There is a rose in every person. If we chose to focus on the good in others, we can all make a difference in the garden."

Not All Roses Bloom On The Same Day

I had an extreme sense of gratitude come over me. I sensed the importance of what Grandma had taught me. I hugged her and said, "Grandma, I will always remember what you've taught me. You have made a difference in me."

She smiled and said, "That means a lot to me Ricky, I'm proud of you."

I smiled back at her.

As I looked at her face, wrinkled and worn by years of life, I thought I saw a tear in her eye.

She put her arm around my shoulder, gave me a little squeeze, and winked at me. Then with a mischievous grin on her face, Grandma asked,

"How about a big piece of chocolate cake?"

Each rose, no matter what color, size, or shape makes a difference and adds beauty to the garden.

The greatest joy you will ever experience is reaching out and lifting others to new heights

Reflection

As I think about the day Grandma's roses bloomed, it reminds me of when I was 30 years old and went into business for myself. I purchased a retail grocery store in Utah. Over the years I owned the store, I learned a lot of different lessons.

I would like to share the most poignant lesson I ever learned in all the years I owned and operated my business. I share this humbly because I feel it's an example of how quickly we can focus on the thorns and forget the rose.

Shortly after buying the store, I hired Burt to be my third man in the store. The idea was that Burt would be one of the managers and ultimately would take on a good share of the responsibility in the store.

Throughout the first year, Burt had difficulty following through with the responsibilities I gave him. It was so bad that some of the other employees were making fun of him. I kept trying to give Burt a chance to take on extra responsibility, but I just couldn't find much that he could follow through on or do to my satisfaction.

Finally it got to the point that his key responsibility was ordering the paper bags along with checking and stocking. It was really quite easy to order paper bags because we had six sizes of bags and they came in bundles. There were six slots in the back room and when we got down to three bundles in a slot he was supposed to order three more.

I got so tired of driving to a neighboring store fifteen miles away to borrow paper bags, I finally felt I needed to let Burt go. The labor expense in the store was out of line, and I felt that Burt was a big part of the problem.

Just after closing one night, I called Burt to the office and I told him I was going to have to let him go. I was 30 years old; Burt was about 45. When I told him I was going to let him go, he sort of slumped down into my office chair and started crying.

I looked at Burt somewhat bewildered. I suggested he go home that night and come back the next day when he could regain his composure and feel more like talking. I also told him I would give him one month's severance pay and would keep him insured until he found another job.

When I went to bed that night, I felt terrible about the situation. I couldn't sleep, so I got out of bed and went into our living room to read. I opened a parenting manual. There was something about Burt's behavior that made me think about what we learned in the parenting class, but I just couldn't put my finger on it.

Not All Roses Bloom On The Same Day

I read the manual twice that night and I came across a principle that really struck home. The principle was that the overall goal of human behavior is to belong or have a sense of belonging.

Furthermore, it follows that if I can't belong in a positive way, I will belong in a negative way. I also read about four ways people can belong in negative ways. The first was attention, the second was power, the third was revenge, and the fourth was display of inadequacy.

As I read about display of inadequacy, I learned that some people belong by being or seeming incapable. It became readily apparent to me that this is how Burt was belonging in the store. The manual suggested that you should stop all criticism, because that is what feeds this misbehavior, and look for ways to give sincere praise. I realized that all Burt was getting was criticism. Praise was nonexistent.

I decided to keep Burt and give him one more chance to succeed. I decided I would put him over my 'no-name' section in the grocery store. No-name products were white label products with similar colored labeling. In other words, they all look exactly alike.

There were two ways to merchandise the no-name products. You could integrate them throughout the store or you could have a solid section. I had chosen to have the solid section. This allowed people interested in no-name products to go to the section and see what no-name products we carried. Then they could shop the rest of the store.

I gave Burt this section because I knew that even if he didn't do it exactly right or if he ordered incorrectly, I could still find a way to praise him honestly. Burt did make some mistakes, but after he was done stocking and facing his section, it was visually perfect. I would praise him and let him know how good his section looked.

After a few months, Burt was doing a really good job. I expanded his responsibilities and assigned him the paper goods section. Again, when he was done stocking, I could go by and compliment him on how good it looked.

After about eight months, I put Burt over the dairy deli section. This is a really difficult section. All of the items in this section are perishable, which means you have to be very careful what you order. It sounds easy, but on the order guide, there's probably a hundred different margarines to pick from. You have to pick the 10 to 20 that you're going to carry and will actually sell in your store. It's a tricky section to manage.

Burt did a great job with the deli section. After about a year, I was feeling really good about myself. I had not fired Burt, he was doing a good job, and I'd done a good thing by keeping him. However, none of this had anything to do with the lesson I was about to learn.

Later that year, Associated Grocers did a store preference survey of our three-county area. We were ranked the most preferred store in the three-county area. This was great, but it was not what caught my attention.

Associated surveyed 350 households. One of the questions they asked was "Why do you prefer to shop at your preferred store?" Fifty-three households named Burt as the reason they shopped the store.

I was blown away. I had been feeling like I had done Burt a favor by keeping him employed, even though the labor was out of line. However, now I could place a value on Burt's contribution to the store. I could simply take a $117, the average family bill, multiplied by 53 households, and that's the revenue Burt was generating each and every week.

I had almost fired Burt because his labor cost was out of line. But Burt's value was hidden in revenues. It couldn't be separated until after the survey. He was actually one of my most valuable employees.

To know Burt was to love him. He was a very gentle and sincere person. He was a good man, and I had almost fired him. I went from feeling magnanimous to feeling extremely humble and fortunate that I had him in my store. What did I learn?

People are valuable. You just need to find out where they are, meet them there, and bring them along.

I am grateful to Burt for the lesson he taught me. A few years ago, Burt passed away. When I attended his services, I saw the lines of people waiting to pay their respects. I saw his children and their spouses showing love and respect to him.

Not All Roses Bloom On The Same Day

Burt taught me that people are valuable. As leaders, we need to remember the most valuable people are those within our own families, classrooms, and companies.

We simply need to find out where they are, meet them there, and bring them along.

People are valuable. You just need to find out where they are, meet them there, and bring them along.

Not All Roses Bloom On The Same Day

Ten Principles of the Rose

1. Not all roses bloom on the same day.

2. One of the greatest strengths a person can have is the ability to see past the thorns and see the rose within.

3. Begin with yourself, clear away the clutter, and focus with faith on the rose within.

4. Faith, love, and patience are three of the most important tools you need to clean your garden and develop the rose within.

5. Discover what people need, and provide for them what they cannot provide for themselves.

6. We all need others to provide for us what we cannot provide for ourselves.

7. Each rose, no matter what color, size, or shape makes a difference and adds beauty to the garden.

8. There is a rose in every person. If we choose to focus on the good in others, we all can make a difference in the garden.

9. People are valuable. You just need to find out where they are, meet them there, and bring them along.

10. The greatest joy you will ever experience is reaching out and lifting others to new heights.

People Who Overcame and Made A Difference

Helen Keller (1880-1968) was born in Tusculum, Alabama. When she was only 19 months old, she experienced a severe childhood illness which left her deaf and blind. She advanced the issues of social welfare, women's suffrage, and disability rights.

Albert Einstein (1879-1955) was a Nobel Prize winning physicist. His intellectual achievements have made the name "Einstein" synonymous with genius. He was slow in learning how to speak. He was rebellious toward authority. A headmaster expelled him. Another said he would never amount to much. He wore loafers because he couldn't tie his shoe laces.

Abraham Lincoln (1809-1865) was elected President of the United States in 1861. He was born in Hardin County, Kentucky. His family upbringing was modest; his parents were from Virginia and were neither wealthy nor well known. He lost his mother when he was very young.

Thomas Edison (1847-1931) was an American inventor and businessman who developed and made commercially available many key inventions. His Edison Electric company was a pioneering company for delivering electricity directly into people's homes. He was largely disinterested at school and attended only three months of formal education. He irritated his teacher with his repeated questioning and inability to follow instructions.

Not All Roses Bloom On The Same Day

B enjamin Franklin (1706-1790) was a scientist, ambassador, philosopher, statesmen, writer, businessman and celebrated free thinker and wit. He was beaten as a child, and brought up in the family business of candle making, also assisting in his brother's printing shop.

L udwig von Beethoven (1770-1827) is one of the most widely respected composers of classical music. He played a crucial role in the transition from classical to romantic music. In his early 20s, Beethoven experienced a slow deterioration in his hearing, which eventually left him completely deaf.

E leanor Roosevelt (1884-1962) was a wife and political aide of American president F.D. Roosevelt. In her own right, Eleanor made a significant contribution to the field of human rights, a topic she campaigned for throughout her life. She was known for her caring and her advocacy for human and civil rights (not her protruding teeth).

O prah Winfrey (born 1954) is an influential talk show host. She is the first woman to own her own talk show. Oprah had a difficult childhood. She lived in great poverty and often had to dress in potato sacks, for which she was mocked at school.

J.K. Rowling (born 1965) is the author of the phenomenal best-selling Harry Potter series. The volume of sales was so high, it has been credited with leading a revival of reading by children. She wrote the first book as a single mother while living on welfare. Now she is one of most successful self-made women in the world.

Nelson Mandela (1918 – 2013) was a South African political activist who spent over 27 years in prison for his opposition to the apartheid regime. He was later elected the first leader of South Africa. He was awarded the Nobel Peace Prize.

Setting Your Personal Goal

Your Name _____,

Birth date _____.

What is your passion? _____

_____

Set a goal to grow your rose within and make a difference.

_____

_____

_____

The Closer the Sunset, the Clearer I See

The closer the sunset the clearer I see.
A new dawn is waiting, with patience I'll see,
the peace that this moment has gifted.
My hearing and vision for the most part lifted.
Now and again they return and I see,
what a blessing this life has been to me.

Oh I have had trials and challenges for sure,
but in between, the joys have been more.
I have some regrets, it is certainly true,
yet small acts of kindness let the light shine through.
I have been tempted to count the faults of my brothers.
I know what's important, the love I show others.

The critical eye is easy to find.
It is harder, by far, to sort of be blind.
Soft eyes allow for others to grow,
and help find the goodness, you may never know.
Kindness finds the path to a better way.
Goodness shines through, at the end of the day.

With grateful heart, I count my blessings each day.
I know, in an instant, my life can go 'way.
So the message I leave is short, and is sweet.
Look around and enjoy the life at your feet.
The closer the sunset the clearer I see.
The love that I give comes back to me.

by Rick Dove

About The Author

Rick Dove is an Emeritus Professor in Professional Sales at Weber State University in Ogden, Utah. He and his wife Mary live in Ogden where they enjoy spending time with their family, especially their 13 grandchildren.

Rick's unique ability to use real life stories to help audiences relate to the principles he teaches has captivated audiences in education and industry.

Rick has years of experience consulting and training on team leadership. Rick is an expert in situational leadership, customer service, building trust, cohesiveness, and improving team performance.

Rick is a Blanchard Channel Partner and recently received a 25-year award from Ken Blanchard.

For training or speaking you can contact Rick at:

Phone: 801-458-6240
Email: focusontherose@gmail.com
Twitter: Rick L Dove @rickldove
Order the book at:
https://www.focusontherose.com
https://www.linkedin.com/in/rickdoveonline/

References

The Parable of the Rose – Author Unknown

Display of Inadequacy – page 34
Don Dinkmeyer Jr. (Author) *The Parent's Handbook: Systematic Training for Effective Parenting Paperback – August 1, 2007*
Don Dinkmeyer Sr. Gary D McKay and Dinkmeyer Jr.
Highly Recommended for Parents and Leaders

Biography Online
Biographies written Tejvan Pettinger
www.biographyonline.net/

www.ingramcontent.com/pod-product-compliance
Lightning Source LLC
Chambersburg PA
CBHW060035050426